ICONS-MARKS-SEALS-TATTOOS-IMAGES-SYMBOLS-VISIONS-SIGNS

By
Dennis D. Helton

ISBN 979-8-9866583-6-0

All Scripture quotes are from the King James Bible

Address All Inquiries To:
THE OLD PATHS PUBLICATIONS, Inc.
142 Gold Flume Way
Cleveland, Georgia, U.S.A.

Web: www.theoldpathspublications.com
E-mail: TOP@theoldpathspublications.com

DEDICATION

This work is dedicated to H.D. Williams and Patricia Williams of The Old Paths Publications, my publishers.

TABLE OF CONTENTS

INTRODUCTION

When did the iconic age begin?

When did the iconic age begin? The definition of iconic is "of, or having the nature of, an icon, image, figure, mark, signs, or representation." Every generation from the beginning of time has had its icons, marks, and images. We can begin with early man and Cain's mark; proceed to present day icons, marks, and relics; and then on to the image of the beast of the Tribulation period.

CHAPTER 1

SEALS & MARKS IN THE OT

Cain's mark

There was an express law prohibiting murder (**Genesis** 9:6; **Exodus** 20:13; 21:12; **Leviticus** 24:21; **Numbers** 35:18; **Deuteronomy** 19:21), but it had not yet been given to early man. However, God personally took care of Cain's punishment (**Genesis** 4:13, 14) by setting a mark upon him (a societal stigmatism). Cain's mark was a great burden to bear for he was in dishonor continually before all and feared he would be slain.

Apparently, Cain sought to lessen the stigmatic mark by moving away to Nod where he was lesser known. He soon married.

- ➤ <u>**What was the mark on Cain?**</u>

There is much speculation as to, "What was the mark on Cain?" Of course, the Bible does not specifically reveal that to us. Most Bible students think it was some sort of indelible marking upon Cain's skin that identified him as a murderer to all that saw him.

To the writer, an outward marking of sorts appears to be a fair assumption. There are many guesses as to Cain's mark. The reader's guess is probably as good as anyones.

CHAPTER 2

JEWISH CONSIDERATIONS

God Forbade the Jews to Make Any Icon or Image

Exodus 20:4: Thou shalt not make unto thee any graven image, or any likeness of any thing that is in heaven above, or that is in the earth beneath, or that is in the water under the earth.

They were not to even make an image of the true God Himself! God hates an image (Deuteronomy 16:22; 4:16; Isaiah 40:15,18; 44:19). Making an image is called changing the truth of God into a lie in Romans 1:25. An image implies that God is constrained in a body and is finite. God is an infinite Spirit (Habakkuk 2:18). Exodus 20:4 does not appear necessarily to be a prohibition against pictures in general but against an attempt to replace worship of the Creator. It does bring into question statues and painting of

Christ, as well as Mary and angels as objects of veneration (Romans 1:21-25).

In Deuteronomy 4:16-19 we have two kinds of idolatry, images and heavenly bodies.

Catholicism skips the Second Commandment and makes the Tenth Commandment two in order to compensate for deleting the Second Commandment.

> ## The honorable men of Jerusalem

In **Ezekiel 9:3-6**, God told the man clothed with linen to **set a mark** upon the forehead of a remnant of the men of Jerusalem that sigh and that cry for all the abominations that be done that they might not be slain with the rest of the city.

> *Ezekiel 9:4: And the LORD said unto him, Go through the midst of the city, through the midst of Jerusalem, and set a mark upon the foreheads of the men that sigh and that cry for all the abominations that be done in the midst thereof.*

A remnant of pious Jews who had opposed the abominable idolatry in Israel were marked upon their foreheads and preserved from judgment by the destroying angels (cherubim). The unmarked were to be executed without mercy – old and young, both maids, and little children, and women (Ezekiel 9:4-10).

As in the case of Cain, we are not told what kind of mark was put upon their foreheads.

➤ <u>**The Scarlet Line**</u>

Rahab hid the two spies, saving their lives. She requested of the two spies to give her a true **token** that kindness would be shown unto her father's house and deliver their lives from death when Israel would come to conquer Jericho. Their reply is in Joshua chapter 2.

> ***Joshua 2:18-19:*** *Behold, when we come in the land, thou shalt bind this line of **scarlet thread** in the window which thou didst let us down by: and thou shalt bring thy father and thy mother, and thy brethren and all thy father's household, home unto thee. And it shall be, that whosoever shall go out of the doors of thy house in to the street, his blood shall be upon his head, and we will be guiltless: and whosoever shall be with thee in the house, his blood shall be on our head, if any hand be upon him.*

This scarlet thread was a sign, badge, or icon representative of their guarantee of safety when judgment came. In like manner, being covered by the shed blood of Christ (our scarlet thread) is a sure safety for the soul when the judgment of God is poured out upon mankind. That scarlet thread runs throughout the Bible like other types, signs, similitudes.

> ***Hosea 12:10** I have also spoken by the prophets, and I have multiplied visions, and used similitudes, by the ministry of the prophets.*

➤ <u>Circumcision</u>

> ***Romans 4:11-12:** And he (Abraham) received the **sign of circumcision, a seal of the righteousness of the faith** which he had yet being uncircumcised: that he might be the father of all them that believe, though they be not circumcised; that righteousness might be imputed unto them also.*

In like manner to the New Testament ordinance of water baptism, circumcision was to the Jews a seal and **sign of faith in God**. However, this did not mean that all who were circumcised were true believers (just as all that are baptized or not true believers).

> ***Romans 2:28-29:** For he is not a Jew, which is one outwardly; neither is that circumcision, which is outward in the flesh: But he is a Jew, which is one inwardly; and **circumcision is that of the heart**, in the spirit, and not in the letter; whose praise is not of men, but of God.*

➤ <u>Tattoo</u>

(The following comments were found on "The Way of Life's webpage in an article titled, "Tattooing for Jesus. Tattooing For Jesus (wayoflife.org)

"**A** survey in Canada found that "75% of young conservative Christians believe tattooing is a valid spiritual expression" ("For the Love of God," *The Vancouver Sun*, Vancouver, British Columbia, February 1999).

"Reporter Douglas Todd of*The Vancouver Sun* visited the Vineyard Christian Fellowship in Langley, British Columbia, and found that tattoos are the newest "in thing" for Vineyard Christians. Amy Bonde, who is a staff member at the Vineyard in Langley, has a large Celtic cross tattooed on the small of her back. Encircling the cross are Hebrew letters that allegedly mean, "I am my beloved's, and he is mine." Bonde says the tattoo signifies that she looks upon Jesus Christ as her "lover."

"*The Vancouver Sun* report notes that the TATTOOING REPRESENTS "A SIGN OF A SEISMIC SHIFT IN EVANGELICAL CHRISTIANITY, which has been associated for most of this century with harsh rules about controlling one's body: no long hair on men, no pants on women, no drinking, no dancing, no jewelry and certainly no tattooing."

"The *Bismarck Tribune* (North Dakota) ran an article in November 1998 about the Christian Tattoo Association operated by

Randy Mastre and two other members of New Song Community Church in Bismarck. Their goal is "to bring Christianity to tattooers." What is wrong with "Christian" tattooing?

First of all, the Old Testament plainly forbade tattooing.

> *"Ye shall not make any cuttings in your flesh for the dead, nor print any marks upon you: I am the LORD" (Lev. 19:28).*

> *"They shall not make baldness upon their head, neither shall they shave off the corner of their beard, nor make any cuttings in their flesh" (Lev. 21:5).*

"This is such a clear command, that one would need a compelling reason to disregard it, even though it is an Old Testament law.

"In some cases we are told in the New Testament that something in the Old is not for us. That is true for the Old Testament dietary laws (Rom. 14:2-3; 1 Tim. 4:1-5) and for the sabbath (Col. 2:16), but there is no such statement in regard to tattooing.

"For a Christian to get a tattoo would be to say that he or she can be certain that what God was concerned about in Leviticus 19:28 and 21:5 He no longer cares about, and I don't see what basis of interpretation allows that.

Second, God's people are not to be identified with evil.

"God forbade the Israelites to cut their flesh because it was an identification with paganism and idolatry, and the New Testament contains the same principles and restrictions.

> *"Abstain from all appearance of evil" (1 Thessalonians 5:22)*

> *"And have no fellowship with the unfruitful works of darkness, but rather reprove them" (Ephesians 5:11).*

> *"I beseech you therefore, brethren, by the mercies of God, that ye present your bodies a living sacrifice, holy, acceptable unto God, which is your reasonable service. And be not conformed to this world..." (Romans 12:1-2).*

> *"But I say, that the things which the Gentiles sacrifice, they sacrifice to devils, and not to God: and I would not that ye should have fellowship with devils. Ye cannot drink the cup of the Lord, and the cup of devils: ye cannot be partakers of the Lord's table, and of the table of devils. Do we provoke the Lord to jealousy? are we stronger than he?" (1 Corinthians 10:20-22).*

"Tattoo' originated from 'tatau' or 'tatu,' which were body markings originally associated with natives, aborigines, cannibals and headhunters of Southeast Asian islands, such as: Polynesia, Micronesia, Samoa, Tahiti, Tonga, New Zealand, New Guinea, Malagasy, and the Marquesas Islands. 'Tattoo' was first mentioned by naturalist Joseph Banks, who accompanied Captain James Cook on the ship *HMS Endeavour* as he explored the Pacific, 1768-1771: 'I shall now mention the way they mark themselves indelibly, each of them is so marked by their humour or disposition.' Sailors brought tattoos to port cities around the world, where, for a century, they were associated with salty sailors, rough working men, slaves, convicts, and circus sideshows" (Bill Federer, "Herman Melville's Classic Novel Moby Dick," *American Minute*).

Tattooing is still intimately associated with idolatry, paganism, moral debauchery, and rebellion.

An article by Clay Thompson in the Pacific News Service for July 27, 1996, was titled "Pagan Fashion's New Frontier - Facial Tattoos." Note that the author, who in this article makes no claim to be a Christian, associates tattoos with paganism. He connects it with a "new reverence for pagan beliefs."

A prominent book on tattooing is *Pagan Fleshworks*. It is by Maureen Mercury and contains photos by Steve Haworth, identified as "the foremost body modification artist in the United States." "Body modification" is the practice of burning, inking, cutting, piercing, and otherwise desecrating one's God-given body.

A July 2003 survey of more than 2,000 people in the United States, reported in the AFP for Oct. 11, found that among women who get tattoos, 34% "feel sexier," and 29% overall "FEEL MORE REBELLIOUS." One woman interviewed by the *Vancouver Sun* admitted that she got a tattoo "PARTLY OUT OF REBELLION against the normal Christian stereotype of 'You can't do this, you can't do that.'" She admits that her mother did not want her to get a tattoo and did not like it ("For the Love of God," *The Vancouver Sun*, Vancouver, British Columbia, Feb. 1999). Another Vineyard member, Peter Davyduck, who has a tattoo of the word "SIN" on his ankle, says this is a message to "judgmental Christians that everyone is a sinner and should be accepted in spite of it." Note the rebellious attitude in this statement. Every born-again Bible-believing Christian knows that everyone is a sinner, but this does not mean that it does not matter how professing Christians should live.

Such rebellion is forbidden in God's Word.

1 Peter 4:5 says,

> *"Likewise, ye younger, submit yourselves unto the elder. Yea, all of you be subject one to another, and be clothed with humility: for God resisteth the proud, and giveth grace to the humble."*

And Ephesians 5:21 says,

> *"Submitting yourselves one to another in the fear of God."*

A young woman who got tattoos before she was saved told me that tattooing is addictive. Wherein is the addiction?

A third reason against tattoos is that the Bible warns the Christian not to cause moral offence and spiritual stumbling.

> *"Give none offence, neither to the Jews, nor to the Gentiles, nor to the church of God"* (1 Cor. 10:32).

> *"Giving no offence in any thing, that the ministry be not blamed"* (2 Cor. 6:3).

> *"Wherefore, if meat make my brother to offend, I will eat no flesh while the world standeth, lest I make my brother to offend"* (1 Cor. 8:10).

This was one of the apostle Paul's guiding principles. He did not want his actions to cause someone to be offended and to stumble spiritually. For this purpose, he was willing even to forego lawful things such as eating meat. How much more should Christians in this age forego highly questionable things such as tattooing and pants on women and "Christian" rock for the sake of being a blessing and encouragement to their conservative brethren! But, sadly, the Christian rock-tattooing culture comes decked out with the rock & roll attitude of "no one is going to take away my fun; I'm not going to let some old fogy tell me what to do."

This is an unscriptural attitude, to say the least. What if a professing Christian follows the example of the "Christian tattoo crowd" and gets involved in the tattoo culture and is drawn into sin?

Not only is the Christian to avoid things that are obviously evil, but he is to avoid things that would cause offense to others even if those things are in not necessarily wrong in themselves:

> *"It is good neither to eat flesh, nor to drink wine, nor any thing whereby thy brother stumbleth, or is offended, or is made weak"* *(Romans 14:21).*

The Christian is to live his life to please others instead of himself. Contemporary-style Christians, though, do not care if they offend others with their rock music and worldly appearance. They protest that they have liberty to do as they please. This is carnal rebellion, and it is the attitude that lies at the heart of apostasy. Those who desire to throw off restrictions on their lifestyles are not following the Bible but their own self-willed lusts.

They are fulfilling 2 Timothy 4:3-4:

"For the time will come when they will not endure sound doctrine; but AFTER THEIR OWN LUSTS shall they heap to themselves teachers, having itching ears; And they shall turn away their ears from the truth, and shall be turned unto fables."

A final reason against tattooing is that the believer's body is not his own; it is the temple of the Holy Spirit.

"What? know ye not that your body is the temple of the Holy Ghost which is in you, which ye have of God, and ye are not your own?" (1 Corinthians 6:19).

For the born-again Christian, tattooing is graffiti on someone's else's temple.

The following is a testimony of Pastor Charlie Haddad who got tattoos before he was saved:

"I was a professing Christian for 24 Years (Catholic) and growing up I was hanging out with some Muslim friends. Some of them got tattoos of a sword and the moon. I then thought I wanted to get a cross and the face of Jesus, and I did, one on each shoulder. Looking back I got them out of pride, it was more of religious pride. I was a Christian only by name, thinking these tattoos would identify me as a Christian, far from it, I didn't know the Lord. Had I really known the Lord and wanted to walk in His ways and the way of His Word I would have obeyed Him and written His Word upon my heart and not on my body. I would have memorized and mediated on His Word instead of having a form of godliness (Proverbs 3:3; 7:2-2). I regret getting these tattoos, and I am ashamed. I know it is not pleasing to the Lord."

Doesn't the Bible say that Jesus has a tattoo on His thigh in Revelation 19:16?

"And he hath on his vesture and on his thigh a name written, KING OF KINGS, AND LORD OF LORDS."

In Revelation 1, Christ is clothed with a garment down to the foot. No one can see His thigh.

[This article is enlarged from *Dressing from the Lord*, which is available from Way of Life Literature, www.wayoflife.org.]

CHAPTER 3

SEALS OR MARKS IN THE NT

<u>Water baptism</u> is the seal or sign of a New Testament believer (Matthew 28:19).

> ***Matthew 28:19*** *Go ye therefore, and teach all nations, baptizing them in the name of the Father, and of the Son, and of the Holy Ghost:*

> ***Romans 6:3*** *Know ye not, that so many of us as were baptized into Jesus Christ were baptized into his death?* ***4*** *Therefore we are buried with him by baptism into death: that **<u>like</u>** as Christ was raised up from the dead by the glory of the Father, even so we also should walk in newness of life.* ***5*** *For if we have been planted together in the **<u>likeness</u>** of his death, we shall be also in the likeness of his resurrection:*

➤ **<u>The 144,000 Tribulation Jews</u>**

The 144,000 Tribulation Jews in Revelation is a remnant of Jewish servants of God. The 144,000 will be **sealed in their foreheads (Revelation 7:3, 4; 14:1, 5)** during The Great Tribulation. These servants are 12,000 Jews from each of the twelve tribes of Israel (not an elect number of people from the modern cult of Jehovah Witness as falsely claimed by them). Some believe that these sealed servants (since no guile is found in them) are ordained to preach the Gospel of the Kingdom to the whole world.

> ***Revelation 7:3:*** *Saying, Hurt not the earth, neither the sea, nor the trees, till we have **sealed** the servants of our God **in their foreheads**.*

➢ The servants of God in Revelation 22

The servants of God in Revelation 22 have the Lamb's name in their forehead.

> ***Revelation 22:4****: And they shall see his face; and his name shall be in their foreheads.*

The locusts that came out of the smoke upon the earth as scorpions were commanded to hurt only those men which have not the seal of God in their foreheads:

> ***Revelation 9:4:*** *And it was commanded them that they should not hurt the grass of the earth, neither any green thing, neither any tree; but only those men which have not **the seal of God in their foreheads**.*

➢ In I Corinthians, "other tongues or languages" was a sign to unbelieving Jews:

> *I Corinthians 14:22: Wherefore **tongues
> are for a sign**, not to them that believe, but
> **to them that believe not**: but prophesying
> serveth not to them that believe not, but for
> them which believe.*

Prophesying (or preaching) was for those that were believers; tongues were a sign at that time in history for unbelievers. Believers at that time in history did not require a sign of tongues because they were convinced and were already believers. Neither do New Testament believers of today require a sign. We have God's Word and preachers and teachers to declare it.

➢ The Jews were slow to believe and required a sign from God:

> *I Corinthians 1:22, 23: For the Jews
> require a **sign**, and the Greeks seek after
> wisdom: But we preach Christ crucified,
> unto the Jews a stumbling block and unto
> the Greeks foolishness.*

In Matthew's Gospel, Jesus chided the Jewish Pharisees and the Sadducees for desiring to be shown a sign:

> *Matthew 16:4: A wicked and adulterous
> generation seeketh after a **sign**, and there
> shall no sign be given unto it, but the sign of
> the prophet Jonas. And he left them, and
> departed*

It appears that Christ knew that these unbelieving Jews would not believe and He left them "as hopeless."

➤ **<u>Mark of the Beast</u>**

The great imitator antichrist personage causes all to receive a mark in their right hand or in their forehead…and his number is six hundred threescore and six (Revelation 13:16, 18).

> **Revelation 13:16:** And he causeth **all**, both small and great, rich and poor, free and bond, to receive <u>a mark</u> **in** their right hand, or **in** their foreheads.

("Global" or "all" has become one of the most prominent words today in economics, religion, and politics)

The reader may have noticed that the word "in" was boldfaced in the verse above. **Dr. Carl Sanders**, developer of the hypodermically inserted "Positive Identification Microchip," now warns Christian audiences that new bible versions will deceive many, as they did him, into believing that the forbidden mark is "on," not "in," the hand or forehead. The King James Bible is the only translation to properly translate Revelation 13:16 with "in" rather than "on." NIV, RSV, and NKJV all translate with "on."

NIV: He also forced everyone, small and great, rich and poor, free and slave, to receive a mark **on** his right hand or **on** his forehead – Revelation 13:16.

RSV: Also it causes all, both small and great, both rich and poor, both free and slave, to be marked **on** the right or the forehead – Revelation 13:16.

NKJV: He causes all, both small and great, rich and poor, free and slave, to receive a mark **on** their right hand or **on** their foreheads – Revelation 13:16.

> ***KJV:*** *And he causeth all, both small and great, rich and poor, free and bond, to receive a mark **in** their right hand, or **in** their foreheads – Revelation 13:16.*

The Greek "epi" can be translated, "on," "upon," "at," "before," and rare cases "in" as found in Romans 6:21 and Titus 1:2. Marks "on" the surface could easily be duplicated and used fraudulently.

A microchip embedded under the skin easily allows the "Big Brother" monitors to locate anyone on earth by satellite tracking. The "underskin" ID Chip is ready now.

In contrast to the Old Testament economy when God gave signs to His national people Israel, New Testament believers are not to live by signs, but by faith.

> ***Romans 5:1, 2:*** *Therefore being justified **by faith**, we have peace with God through our Lord Jesus Christ. By whom also we have*

*access **by faith** into this grace wherein we stand, and rejoice in hope of the glory of God.*

***Hebrews 4:2:** For unto us was the gospel preached, as well as unto them (Israel): but the word preached did not profit them, **not being mixed with faith** in them that heard it.*

The Jews sought for **signs** and **miracles.**

***Matthew 12:38** Then certain of the scribes and of the Pharisees answered, saying, Master, we would see a sign from thee. **39** But he answered and said unto them, An evil and adulterous generation seeketh after a sign; and there shall no sign be given to it, but the sign of the prophet Jonas:*

But

***Hebrews 11:6**: But without **faith** it is impossible to please him: for he that cometh to God must **believe** that he is, and that he is a rewarder of them that diligently seek him.*

The Old Testament is replete with signs: Ezekiel 20:12; 31:13-17; Numbers 16:38; Deuteronomy 6:8; Joshua 4:6; I Samuel 2:34; 2 Kings 19:29; Isaiah 7:11; 19:20; 20:3; 37:30; 55:13; Jeremiah 44:29.

CHAPTER 4

CONTEMPORARY MARKS, NUMBERS, AND SPOTS

False signs from false prophet

Some of the **NKJV's** (New King James Version) sport the number 666 in the form of a **mobius** on its covers. The most popular New Age magazine "Aquarian Conspiracy" also has the same symbol.

➤ **<u>Mobius</u>**

(**mobius** = a one-side surface constructed from a rectangle by holding one end fixed and rotating the opposite end 180 degrees and applying it to the first end. This symbol is recognized by Luciferians. There is a Mobius Group in Los Angeles which is a leader in investigating psychic phenomena. Some New Agers claim the modius symbolizes the Holy Trinity)

- Many Roman Catholics put **spots** on their <u>forehead</u> on their Ash Wednesday service.
- Hindu Krishna devotees don daily doses of <u>cow excrement</u> <u>on their forehead</u>.
- The point-bindu is a standard religious symbol throughout the world...bindi, the red **spot** that Hindu women wear <u>on their forehead</u>.
- Buddhists worldwide revere effigies of Gautama Buddha and Buddhist saints with a **mark** on their <u>forehead</u> and on their <u>hand</u>
- An image of 'the Virgin' appearing in Marienfried, Germany to Barbara Reuss, speaks, calling for the taking of **a mark** on the <u>forehead</u>. This phantom pronounces to all: *I am the Sign of the living God. I place my sign on the forehead of my children* (*Mystery Mark of the New Age*, p. 52).

Visions, apparitions, and icons of the Mary of Roman Catholicism

- The Catholic Church attempts to deify Mary by capitalizing the word "virgin" when referring to her. New Age Bibles such as the NIV do the same.
- **NIV** omits **Luke 1:28**...blessed art thou among women. NIV capitalizes "virgin" to allow possibilities such as perpetual

virginity for Mary – (**2 Kings** 19:21; **Isaiah** 23:12; 37:22; 47:1; **Jeremiah** 18:13; 31:4; 31:21; 46:11; **Lamentations** 1:15; 2:13; **Amos** 5:2).

- The Catholic Council of Chalcedon in AD 451 proclaimed Mary's perpetual virginity.

- Many Catholics pray to Mary instead of praying to God. The virgin or mother goddess has perennially been the tangible icon through which that nature god has been addressed and venerated. An engraving on a goddess icon from ancient Egypt reads, "I am all that has been, or that is, or that shall be." – (Alexander Hislop, *The Two Babylons*, p. 7).

This Mary is not the Mary of the Bible.

Note: Mary worship was established by Cardinal Benedetto Odescalchi, the first pope with the name of Innocent XI, when he initiated THE WORSHIP OF THE IMAGE, placed on the altar in 1677, and wanted his heart to be buried here, not in the main chapel. This is placed on a plaque in the Chapel of the Virgin of the Grace at Saints Vincent and Anastasius.

➢ <u>Visions of Benny Hinn:</u>

(The following excerpts concerning **Benny Hinn** are taken from, *The Bible For Today*, B.F.T. #2784, October-December 1997, *"Benny Hinn's Move Into Necromancy,"* by Richard Fisher with M. Kurt Goedelman)

Hinn has long been infatuated with the late faith healer, **Kathryn Kuhlman**. In his "Partner Conference" in Atlanta and to those viewing the June 11, 1997 installment of his daily "This is Your Day" program, he stated "The Lord showed me a vision...I saw myself walk into a room and there stood **Kathryn Kuhlman**...she said, 'Follow me'...And I followed her to a second room. In that second room stood the Lord...when I saw the Lord, **Kathryn** disappeared...And now the Lord looked at me and said, 'Follow me.' And I followed him to a third room. In the third room sat a gentleman...in this wheelchair...a big hole in his neck...A tube down his throat...tubes down his body. Totally crippled...paralyzed...And now as the man was healed, the Lord looked at me with piercing eyes and said, Do it!'...and the dream and the vision came to an end...It was **Kathryn Kuhlman** who took me, who introduced me to the Holy Spirit.

In <u>Hinn's</u> Honolulu Crusade, he lured the audience with his revelations of not only Kuhlman but the Old Testament prophet **Elijah**. "I have not just seen angels, I've seen saints"**...**I've walked in the supernatural world**...**I've had individuals appear to me in my room. Not only **angels...**I was in prayer one day and a man appeared in front of me...And I spoke out and I said, 'Lord, who is this man I see?**...**I know you may---you may think I lost my mind, but the Lord said, 'Elijah the prophet.'

If we believe Hinn's words, it appears that he has had more visions than "John the Revelator."

In Orlando on December 31, 1989, Hinn said, "**The mid '90s** will see a new move of God to shake the world with the last great revival. **Many will be raised from the dead**. Angels will come knocking at your door...An earthquake will hit the east coast of America and destroy much in the '90s. Not one place will be safe in America from earthquakes in the '90s."

<u>The following is taken from *The Voice in the Wilderness* monthly publication, pp. 4, 5, February 2002, P.O. Box 7037, Asheville, NC 28802:</u>

A man Hinn had "slain in the Spirit" fell on a prostrate elderly woman and broke her hip, resulting in her death.

At a South Africa crusade a man collapsed; Hinn said the Lord told him the man would be okay, but he died in the ambulance.

In 1993 in Basel, Switzerland, Hinn prophesied over a man with cancer that he had many years to live. He died two days later.

In Nairobi, Kenya early in May 2000, four patients released from a hospital to attend Hinn's "Miracle Crusade" died while waiting for prayer.

In a guttural voice, **Hinn curses those who dare to question him**, curses their children and threaten that if he had a "Holy Ghost machine gun" he'd "mow down" critics.

According to the *The Voice in the Wilderness*, Benny **Hinn scorned doctrine as "sick stuff"** and said, "I don"t discuss doctrine." Even TBN's **Paul Crouch** referred to sound doctrine as "doctrinal doodoo."

(**Note:** If you do not have **doctrine**, you do not have a foundation - **Proverbs** 4:2; **Isaiah** 28:9; 29:24; **Matthew** 7:28; **Mark** 1:22; 4:2; 12:38; **Luke** 4:32; **John** 7:17; **Acts** 2:42; 5:28; 13:12; **Romans** 6:17; **I Corinthians** 14:6; **I Timothy** 1:3, 10; 4:6, 13, 16; 5:17; 6:1, 3; **2 Timothy** 3:16; 4:2, 3; **Titus** 1:9; 2:1, 7, 10; **2 John** 9-10. The virgin birth of Christ and His Deity is doctrine. The reality of Heaven and Hell is doctrine. The Second

Coming of Christ is doctrine. Any biblical truth is doctrine.)

Ancient Israel had the same problems with false prophets and false visions even as we do today:

> ***Ezekiel 13:3:*** *Thus saith the Lord GOD; Woe unto the foolish prophets, that follow their own spirit, and have seen nothing!*
>
> ***Ezekiel 13:6-7:*** *They have seen vanity and lying divination, saying, The LORD saith: and the LORD hath not sent them: and they have made others to hope that they would confirm the word. Have ye not seen a vain vision, and have ye not spoken a lying divination, whereas ye say, The LORD saith it; albeit I have not spoken?*

According to a Dallas-based organization known as *Trinity Foundation*, a watchdog group for televangelist, any time somebody on Hinn's Board of Directors disagrees with Hinn, he changes the board. Trinity Foundation has criticized Hinn for his lavish lifestyle, which includes a $10 million parsonage in California. "Can you imagine...spending $11,000 a night for a hotel room when you're on a side trip and charging it to the ministry?" Trinity Foundation president, Ole Anthony, asks. "Or thousands and thousands of dollars given to his wife and kids to go on shopping sprees? This isn't the way of God's people, " he contends. – (*Agape Press*, Allie Martin, 7/8/2005, http://headllines.agapepress.org/archive/7/72005e.asp)

(The followed copied from *The Voice in the Wilderness*, page 14, May 2005, www.thevoice inthewilderness.org)

<u>Kathryn Kuhlman</u> – In his book Healing: *A Doctor in Search of a Miracle*, **Dr. William Nolen** dedicates an entire chapter to his experiences investigating Kuhlman's healing crusades. Though sympathetic to Kuhlman as a person, Nolen was unable to document medically even one case of physical healing. At the time of his investigation, Dr. Nolen was chief of surgery at Meeker County Hospital in Litchfield, Minnesota.

In his book *Occult ABC*, **Kurt Koch** described his own research into Kuhlman's healing ministry. He carefully followed up on a list of 28 cases of alleged healings in Minneapolis, Minnesota. "Ten had not been healed, seven had experienced an improvement in their condition, eleven had diseases in which the mind can play an important part. In the whole of this extensive report, there is not one clear case of healing from an organic disease" *–fridaynews/wayoflife.org/4/4/05*

➤ **<u>Jeane Dixon's visions:</u>**

There are those who counted **Jeanne Dixon's prophecies** and concluded that she had a prediction accuracy percentage rate that was lower than most Wall Street stock brokers.

Jeanne luckily (or with the assistance of demons) and accurately predicted some major events: -*Jeane Dixon: The Washington Prophetess*, By Noel Smith:

In 1966 she told a newspaper reporter that Jawaharial Nehru would be succeeded as Prime Minister of India within approximately seven years by a man whose name began with the letter "S." On May 27, 1964, the intellectual Nehru died, and he was succeeded by Lal Bahadur Shastri.

In 1952 Mrs. Dixon described the President who would be elected in 1960. The description fit John F. Kennedy, and perfectly. And she predicted that that President would die a violent death while in office. She predicted that President Kennedy would be shot while in office; and she vainly sought to persuade some of his friends to get him to cancel his trip to Texas.

In June 1953 she said that Chief Justice Fred M. Vinson would die within a few months. He died suddenly the following September.

On June 19, 1964, she saw another tragedy in the Kennedy family. She vainly tried to persuade friends of Senator Ted Kennedy to keep him out of airplanes. A plane in which he was a passenger crashed on that day, and we all know the tragic consequences to the Senator.

In December 1963, when the strutting Nikita Khrushchev was to all appearances the master of Soviet Russian and her slave states, and would continue to be the master as long as the scoundrel wished, Mrs. Dixon said that Khrushchev would "shortly" be disposed. He was disposed the following October, and he has remained disposed. Since that October we haven't heard so much as a squeak form him.

In the fall of 1944 Franklin D. Roosevelt asked Mrs. Dixon to come to the White House. He asked her how much time he had left to finish his work. She told him six months or less. He died at Warm Springs, Georgia, on April 12, 1945.

When Prime Minister Winston Churchill was in Washington on an official visit in 1945, Mrs. Dixon told him that if he called the election that he had decided to call, he would be turned out of office. But she also told him that after six years he would be back as Prime Minister. "England will never let me down," he replied in the gruff Churchillian manner. Churchill called the election.

England turned him out and put Clem Attlee in. Six years later Churchill was again Prime Minister.

In 1962 Mrs. Dixon said that Churchill would die at the end of 1964. She missed it twenty-six days.

She told Vice President Harry Truman that he would become President "through an act of God."

Mrs. Dixon said that the "symbols" told her that Fidel Castro believed that President Kennedy and Khrushchev were planning to eliminate him and replace him with somebody more to the liking of the United States and the United Nations. Therefore, Castro arranged the assassination and Oswald was his triggerman. She said that others were involved in the plot.

<u>She also missed quite a few. Mrs. Dixon admitted that her predictions are not always correct.</u>

<u>EXAMPLES</u>:
- ✓ She predicted that World War III would begin in 1954.
- ✓ Red China would be admitted to the United Nations in 1958, yet this did not occur until 1971.
- ✓ The Vietnam War would end in 1966, yet it did not end until 1975.

✓ She predicted that Union Leader, Walter Reuther, would run for President in 1964, which he did not do.

✓ Jeane predicted that Castro would be overthrown from Cuba in 1970.

✓ Jeane predicted that Russia would be the first nation to put a man on the moon.

✓ On October 19, 1968, she predicted Jacqueline Kennedy was not thinking of marriage and the next day Mrs. Kennedy married Aristotle Onassis.

(McDowell & Stewart, *Handbook of Today's Religions*," pp. 183-184, Thomas Nelson Publishers, 1983.)

<u>Jeane Dixon speaks nothing about the Lord Jesus Christ, nor sin, salvation, and judgment</u>

Mrs. Dixon, a devout Roman Catholic, said that during her visions she is "so filled with the glory of God" that she wants to give everything to everyone. She believed that her powers were a gift from God and refers to Paul's words in First Corinthians 12:4-11.

Mrs. Dixon didn't begin her career as a prophetess on her knees before God, with the open Bible as her guide. She began it at the steps of the covered wagon of a gypsy fortune-teller, with a crystal ball as her guide.

Mrs. Dixon has nothing to say about Jesus Christ, The Son of God, the "image of the invisible God, the first born of every creature."

Mrs. Dixon has nothing to say about Christ's substitutionary death, nothing to say about the absolute necessity of that death, nothing to say about His resurrection, nothing to say about His ascension. Nothing at all about Jesus Christ.

Jesus Christ is the central theme of the prophets of God. Jesus Christ is the central theme of both the Old and New Testaments. And His substitutionary death for sinners is the center of the central theme.

It only takes one of Jeane Dixon's **visions** to set off an alarm bell:

It is in Washington shortly after a humid midnight on July 14, 1952. Mrs. Dixon is in bed, "drowsy but not asleep." She has a sheet across her body. Suddenly she feels a motion against the mattress "to the left of my head." She rolls onto the left side, facing the east. She sees the body, but neither the head or tail, of a snake. It is "no bigger around than a garden hose." She feels the "powerful little body: twisting down the side of her bed and raising the mattress at the foot. She seems "cloaked in a substance as soft as eiderdown." She feels the snake's head "nudging" beneath her ankles. Its body grows larger as it wraps itself around her legs and hips. The snake gradually entwines itself around her chest. She sees its head but not the eyes. The snake has become about as "big around as a man's arm." The snake slowly turns its eyes and gazes into Mrs. Dixon's. "In them was the all-knowing wisdom of the ages." The snake is "vividly colored in yellow and black," has great jowls "like miniature pyramids." The snake turns its eyes toward the east, and then turns its eyes toward Mrs. Dixon..."I sensed that it was telling me that if my faith was great enough I could penetrate some of this divine wisdom. I knew that I had God's protection, for the steady gaze of the reptile was permeated with love, goodness, strength, and knowledge. A sense of 'peace on earth, good will toward men's coursed through my being.

The Bible tells us about another lady deceived by the serpent in the Book of Genesis. God has not called angels, apostates, nor snakes to reveal prophecy to us. His Words are finalized in the Book of Revelation. See Hebrews 1:2; John 1:1-2, 14; Revelation 22:19.

➢ <u>What if the extra-biblical predictions are accurate?</u>

A false prophet (or anyone) may accurately predict events but they must be rejected unless they are meticulously true to Scriptures, giving all honor to Christ as Creator, Savior, and Lord. Besides this, the Scriptures indicate that the prophecies of God received by men directly (future forecasting) would be "done away."

> ***I Corinthians 13:9-10:*** *For we know in part, and we **prophesy** <u>in part</u>. But when that which is perfect is come (completed Scriptures), then that which is <u>in part</u> (sign gifts) shall be **done away**.*

Prophecies remained <u>in part</u> (**I Corinthians 13:10**) until John concluded the book of Revelation. The Word of God contains all of the prophecy that God pleases to reveal to us. Many egotistical "so called" preachers seek spiritual recognition for themselves at the expense of ignoring and making Scriptures of less importance.

> ***I Corinthians 13:8:*** *Charity never faileth: **but whether there be prophecies, they shall fail**; whether there be tongues, they shall cease: whether there be knowledge, it shall vanish away.*

> ***John 4:48:*** *The said Jesus unto him, Except ye see **signs** and wonders, ye will not believe.*

God greatly honors His name (**Psalms 111:9**) but **He magnifies His Word (the Scriptures) above His own Name**

> ***Psalms 138:2:*** *I will worship toward thy holy temple, and praise thy name for thy lovingkindness and for thy truth: for **thou hast magnified thy word above all thy name.***

Anyone may predict the outcome of some events (especially when there are only two outcomes; there is an easy 50:50 chance) but that does not make him or her a prophet or prophetess.

An ingenious scam artist in a large northern city devised a clever scheme to get rich. Using the huge city phone directory, he selected a large pool of names at random and sent them the predicted winner of various events (boxing matches; politics; sporting events; etc.). Half of the pool of names would receive the name of one party and the other half the opposite party. In this way, the scammer would always be correct in half of his predictions (a 50:50 proposition). The scammer would then repeat sending the dual predictions each time only to the winning parties (getting 50% correct every time). Of course, the scammer would request money from those who had received the correct predictions in order for them to receive more "correct" future predictions. Yes, he got caught.

Even a blind hog might root up an acorn every now and then.

➢ How do we identify a false prophet?

Deuteronomy 18:20-22: *But <u>the prophet, which shall presume to speak a word in my name</u>, which I have not commanded him to speak, or that shall speak in the name of other gods, even that prophet shall die. And if thou say in thine heart, How shall we know the word which the LORD hath not spoken? When a prophet speaketh in the name of the LORD, **if the thing follow not, nor come to pass**, that is the thing which the LORD hath not spoken, **but the prophet hath spoken it presumptuously**: thou shalt not be afraid of him.*

Matthew 7:15-16: *Beware of **false prophets**, which <u>come to you in sheep's clothing</u>, but inwardly they are ravening wolves. Ye shall know them <u>by their fruits</u>. Do men gather grapes of thorns or figs of thistles?*

Matthew 15:9: *But in vain they do worship me, teaching for doctrines the commandments of men*

Matthew 24:24: *For there shall arise false Christs, and **false prophets**, and shall shew **great signs and wonders**; insomuch that, if it were possible, they shall deceive the very elect.*

I Peter 2:1: *But there were false prophets also among the people, even <u>as there shall be false teachers among you,</u> who privily (secretly) shall bring in damnable heresies, even denying the Lord that bought them,*

45

and bring upon themselves swift destruction.

__John 4:1:__ Beloved, believe not every spirit, but try the spirits whether they are of God: because __many false prophets__ are gone out into the world.

__John 7:__ Many __deceivers__ are entered into the world, who confess not that Jesus Christ is come in the flesh. This is a deceiver and an antichrist

__Jude 4:__ There are certain men crept in unawares, who were before of old ordained to this condemnation, ungodly men, turning the grace of our God into lasciviousness, and denying the only Lord God, and our Lord Jesus Christ.

There were warnings in the OT against false prophets turning people to other gods - (**Deuteronomy 13:1-5; 18:20-22**).

There were those with familiar spirits that peeped and muttered – **Isaiah 8:19**.

__Isaiah 8:20:__ To the law and to the testimony: if they speak not <u>according to this word</u>, it is because there is no light in them.

➢ **For "True" Believers:**

- There is **no priest but Christ;**
- **No sacrifice but Calvary;**
- **No confessional but the Throne of Grace;**
- **No authority but the Word of God.**

> ***Matthew 7:22-23:*** *Many will say unto me in that day, Lord, Lord, have we not **prophesied in thy name?** and **in thy name have cast out devils?** and **in thy name done many wonderful works?** And then will I profess unto them, **I never knew you**, depart from me, ye that work iniquity.*

This is a shocking expose' of religious people performing miraculous works! God openly exposes their scandalous workings.

> ### <u>Madam Blavatsky (of Theosophy religion) states:</u>

"Imprudent are the Christian theologians who have degraded them into Fallen Angels and now call them Satan and his demons. Is he not. .Sanatsuyala, another name of **Mother...the Celestial Virgin...Mother of the Invisible Universe**, also called the Great Dragon" – (H.P. Blavatsky, *The Secret Doctrine*, Vol. I, London: The Theosophical Publishing Society, 1893, pp. 495-496).

> ### <u>B.F. Westcott</u>

B.F. Westcott agrees with Blavatsky that visions of 'the virgin' are merely God changing "form." (Westcott is the editor of the New Greek text underlying the NIV, NASB and all new bible versions.) Reports of **visions** of virgins and Mary are occurring worldwide.

Visionaries have reported more than 400 "apparitions" of the Virgin in the 20th Century. There is a demonic goddess spirit behind these apparitions. Hundreds of millions are responding to the Mother of the World (Queen of Peace) and are bringing their troubles to the thousands of shrines set up to honor the *so-called* Virgin Mary. The more famous shrines such as Fatima, Lourdes, Guadeloupe, and Medjugoric attract millions of visitors each year.

Arthur **Jim Tetlow**, in his book, *Messages From Heaven*, catalogs tens of thousands of such events. Some are simply tears on a stone statue. Others involve ongoing visions and complex messages from a spectacular apparition. Tetlow says, "The apparitions of a Mary, taken as a whole, portray a powerful, glorious Queen who comes in Christ's name, wielding all His power and attributes. Most of the appearances exhibit similarities. A beautiful lady, robed in light, appears and calls herself Mary, Queen of Heaven, Queen of Peace."

A red trickle from the left eye of a concrete statue of the Virgin Mary at a Vietnamese Catholic Martyrs Church in Sacramento California has attracted a steady stream of visitors hoping for a miracle (*Battle Cry*, Jan/Feb 2006, pp. 1, 2).

Posted on the internet (August 18, 2006) was an article concerning the sighting of Mary in a chocolate dropping. The article said that a nearly perfect image of the Mother of God (how does anyone know how Mary looked) has been formed in a 2-inch-tall chocolate statue found under a vat on August 14, (06) by employees of the California based Bodega Chocolates. The Associated Press reports resemblances to "traditional" depictions of Mary. The tiny figure spent much of the week in the window of the chocolate store gift shop but has now been moved to a safer place out of sight. The chocolate dropping was found on Monday by a kitchen worker who spotted the melted lump of chocolate when she started her shift. The finder, Cruz Jacinto, said, "For me, it was a sign." Don't the Scriptures count for anything? It amazes the writer that people are so gullibly duped by such minor things of little or no important significance. God's Word should have the preeminence. Many times, God's Word condemns images (as a means of adoration and worship): Perhaps the reader might reason that this image of the chocolate dropping was not arbitrarily made. Then why all the stir, awe, and devotion to a chocolate dropping that has no bearing upon God's Word. As for a sign, Jesus said:

*An evil and adulterous generation seeketh after a sign; and there shall no sign be given to it, but the sign of the prophet Jonas (**Matthew 12:39**).*

Exodus 20:4: *Thou shalt not make unto thee **any graven image**, or **any likeness of any thing** that is in heaven above, or that is in the earth beneath, or that is in the water under the earth.*

2 Thessalonians 2:9-12: *Even him, whose coming is after the working of Satan with all power and **signs and lying wonders**, And with all deceivableness of unrighteousness in them that perish; because they received not the love of the truth, that they might be saved. And for this cause God shall send them **strong delusion**, that they should believe a lie: That they all might be damned who believed not the truth, but had pleasure in unrighteousness.*

The title 'The Virgin' has been applied to the goddesses of...

- Canaanites – Astarte and Ashtoreth
- Babylon – Rhea or Semiramis and Baal or Bel (Jeremiah 51:44)
- Egyptians – Isis (goddess mother), Horus (child)
- Hindus – Isi, Kanyabava, Trigana
- Rome – Venus (goddess), Jupiter (child), mother of Romulus and Remus)
- Greco-Roman goddesses – Ceresk Hestisk Vesta, Diana, Artemis, Demeter, and Cybele
- China – Shing Moo (Holy Mother)

- Greece – Aphrodite, The Mediatrix
- India – Devaki (goddess), Crishna (child)
- Ephesus – Diana (the mother of gods identified with Semiramis)
- Scandinavia – Disa (pictured with a child)
- Israel – Ashtaroth (goddess), Baal (child) – Judges 2:13
- Africa – the Great Mother and Child received divine honors
- Catholicism's Mary (not Mary, mother of Jesus, as claimed by the Catholic Church)

➤ **The root of Mary worship:**

Semiramis (sih MIHR uh mihs) was a mythical queen of Assyria who supposedly founded the ancient city of Babylon, and conquered Persia and Egypt. Herotus mentions a Semiramis who was queen of Babylon in the 700's B.C. – World Book Enclyclopedia, Volume 17, p. 235, copyright 1980, USA.

Semiramis became a goddess with many names: Baalti, (The Madonna), The Great Goddess Mother, Queen of Heaven, The Mediatrix, The Mother of Mankind, Astarte, etc.

Alexander Hislop (almost 100 years ago) concluded that 'the Virgin' would be the "image of the beast" worshipped during the great tribulation (*The Two Babylons*, p. 263).

New Age writers concede that this 'virgin' is indeed the Great Dragon which Revelation 20:2 reveals to be Satan.

CHAPTER 5

SYMBOLOGY USED IN FALSE AND SECRET SOCIETIES

Symbology used in Secret Societies

Symbology used in Secret Societies is illustrated by the following excerpts from Gianni DeVincent Hayes, Ph.D, December 30, 2007, *NewsWithViews.com*)

All covert groups, especially the Inner Circle which some refer to as the Illuminati but who are really the core of all societies, have stealth means of conveying messages to each other. Sometimes it's a specific type of handshake; other times it's a coded action, but more often that not, it's shapes or figures or legends. The first group to pop into one's mind is Freemasonry, which operates out of a slew of symbols used for double meanings. The compass, for example, means more than a measuring instrument, as do the cube and the square, among many other symbols.

Most symbols are codified and connected with measurements, math, and numerology. Nearly all have hidden occultic meanings.

Mysticism, witchcraft, cabalism (mystical philosophical doctrine based on the doctrines of a Jewish mystical movement based on a symbolic interpretation of the Scriptures), astronomy and the esoteric (secret inner understanding limited to only a chosen few) all work together, along with concepts of gods and goddesses, femininity and masculinity, and fertility. **Symbology** dates back farther than the Tower of Babylon…if you study history and follow through on certain aspects (i.e. Knights Templar) and certain people (Pike, Blavatsky, and those of even earlier days), you'll see the thread that weaves what appears to be the loose strands. Tie all this in with secret societies, and you have the New World Order…Symbology and secret societies are very sophisticated, and those advancing both want none of us to be aware of them. That's why they operate out of secrecy. And who "they" are apparently are what most refer to as the "Power Elite," or the Illuminati… They have a plan for the world—one that denies humanity, rejects God, destroys right, erodes constitutions, collapses currencies, dumbs-down our children, and creates diseases (?) and other horrors to depopulate our planet while getting fat and wealthy off each of us.

Dr. Hayes quoting Dr. Makow: Dr. Henry Makow says, "Dating back to Zoroastrianism, the Jewish Cabala reverses the roles of God and Lucifer and embraces occult **symbols**, rituals and blood sacrifices. This is the Cosmic Struggle between Spirit and Matter…The Cabalists secretly dedicated themselves to destroying Christianity and Western civilization…In 1773 Amschel Mayer Rothschild convened a meeting of 12 prominent Jewish bankers and other prominent Jewish personalities and submitted a programme to level the social order using the contradictory promise of "liberty: and "equality," In 1776, they had Adam Weishaupt organize the Order of the Illuminati, which merged with Freemasonry in 1782…Freemasonry is Cabala and, in the words of Andre Krylienko, (The Red Thread) it was "launched for the purpose of enlisting non-Jews consciously or unconsciously in the service of Jewry." (p. 93)

Symbols are not accidents. They are tools of the Elite, the Inner Circle and all the groups attached to them.

Symbols to ponder:

➢ <u>Star of David</u>

Star of David is a six-pointed star with two triangles and is Israel's flag. But the occultists see it as a sign of black and white magic. It's connected to Jewish mysticism and is made of two triangles (tri-angles = the number 3). Inside the star, often depicted is an all-seeing eye in a creature that looks like an elephant with a crown on top, and atop that seems to be an upside-down dove. Of the two triangles, the tip of the one that points down denotes femininity, the moon and water. The triangle tip pointing upward depicts sun, fire, and masculinity. "The "empty" hexagram, without crossing lines isn't used in Western ideography except as a form for a policeman's badge in Iceland and in certain states in the US (the sheriff's star)" - (Quote and diagrams by www.syumbol.com).

➢ <u>Yin and Yang</u>

Like the double-headed eagle, this symbol is of dialectics (opposites). It represents equally colored white and black (light and dark) circles, and where the black is, there is a minuscule white dot, and where the white is, there is an equal-sized, teeny, black circle. Opposites integrate to form one unity.

Many of the dialectical symbols also represent the opposites of male and female. Some perceive the separation of black and white by an "S," representing Satan streaming through its diameter. Yin is the female counterpart and is symbolic of dark and negative; yang the white side, is masculine and represents the opposite: light and positive - (Diagrammed by Pastor Billy Bissell).

> ## **Babylon**

Babylon is is found in the Bible when the Babylonians tried to build a tower (Tower of Babel) to reach heaven. It's symbolic for worldly, wealthy, powerful, as it was a great and powerful metropolis for its era, and it considered itself above everyone and everything else, the richest and the best place to live… Some people consider America the modern day Babylon. Today, the word connotes evil behavior, a sinful lifestyle or city. The Babylonian Gardens in Iraq were being re-built by Saddam Hussein; some say through the Illuminati. The Babylonians, as is true with many other nations, worship the sun god. "This structure—maze or labyrinth—is probably a representation of the mythological monster, half human, half bull.

➤ <u>Tower of Babel</u>

If you look up this image in any religious or history book, you'll see its composition is formed by concentric circles…representing a perverted, sadistic civilization that thought they were omnipotent and in contemptuous and conceited union began to build a tower that would reach the heavens.

➤ <u>Druids</u>

"This ancient cult is attributed to having in some manner created Stonehenge. The Druids are also thought to be connected to the Italian horn or unicorn horn, though most related druids to Celtic or Irish ethnicity. "The Druid Sigil is most often rendered as a circle with two vertical lines passing through it. Frequently this is drawn, painted, embroidered, etc. as a wreath of leaves with two staves (or spears for the warrior types) passing through.""

➤ <u>Witches</u>

Their black cape and flying prowess makes them separate from humans and are believed to be in the league with Satan, and thus are considered evil, though some adamantly claim they are white (or good) witches. Scholars of Satanism and witchcraft say there are no white witches…only black, and that they are very real and influential through the use of dark symbols and sinister societies, and the worship of the devil.

➢ <u>Moon Goddess</u>

Moon Goddess is called Goddess Diana. The crescent moon was adopted as a sign of Islam in the 1300's. Later, a star was added to depict sovereignty and divinity. The moon is largely perceived as feminine even though its topography looks like "the man in the moon." This dates back to the myth that a man was nailed to the moon to purge himself of sin. Eclipses of the moon are considered to be evil. Other negative facets include high tidal waves, especially at night (as water is central to mythology), werewolves, and wolves baying at the moon—the darker side of humanity—vampires desiring the moon over the sun. People associate madness, bizarre behavior, lunacy (notice the word "Luna" which means moon in Latin) to the full moon and its cycle (the unending cycle of life—birth, date, and rebirth). Moonstruck people are said to be mad, or madly in love. The Ibis is an Egyptian deity representing the soul and the moon (the feminine side) while birds of prey (hawks, eagles, etc) signify the sun and the masculine side. Thus, the crescent with a star indicates worshippers of prostitution, of the unknown world (Ouija, astrology, spiritualists, fortunetellers and clairvoyants, and other psychics and gazers).

➢ **Eagle**

This sky god represents royalty, power, kingliness, pride, strength, courage, and a ruler; fighter of the serpent, rising sun, and protector, but the slayer of unwitting prey as it espies with its keen eyesight. Eagles serve as symbols, emblems, and other markers. A Double-headed Eagle is representative of the dialectics (opposites) of nature, and is depicted as being pulled in opposite directions. The zodiac sign for Pisces, two fish swimming in opposite directions, is the same. This symbol often is used in occultism.

➢ **Birds**

Crows = Black birds/ravens are credited with evil, being bad omens, forewarning of death. Shintoism sees the black bird as a messenger of god while the Chinese regard it—when coupled with a white heron—as representative of their yin and yang (black and white, dialectical opposites, male and female).

Raven = stands as a messenger of the gods; overall, it's a harbinger of illness, darkness, war, and death.

Swans = feminine, beauty, grace, and the goddess Venus/Aphrodite.

Doves = love and peace, Christianity; seven doves in a circle symbolize the Holy Spirit's seven gifts (God-fearing, wisdom, understanding, counsel, fortitude, knowledge, and piety); It represents the Holy Spirit entering Jesus, and its opposite is often depicted as a raven or vulture.

Falcons = similar to eagles, they represent free spirit, having healing powers, strength, a sacrifice for the sun god, Re (Egyptian), and because of their acute vision, falcons also represent the all-seeing eye of Horus. While these birds are reflection of the masculine side and the sun, the **vulture**—another bird of prey—is seen as feminine in spite of its carnivorous menus, and the consuming of the dead.

➢ <u>**Satan's "S"**</u>

It looks like a double bolt of lightening running vertically. This was the mythical Zeus' weapon, and was worn by the Nazi SS and means "annihilator."

➢ <u>**The peace symbol**</u>

The peace symbol is an inverted cross with broken arms encased within a circle.

➢ **T Sign**

The T Sign is a symbol of Roman Catholic worship

➢ **The "T" sign of the cross**

The "**sign of the cross**" is a **symbol** of Romish worship. No prayer can be said, no worship engaged in, no step can be taken without the frequent use of the sign of the cross. It is a grand **charm** to Catholics and a preserver from the powers of darkness. This same sign of the cross was used in the Babylonians Mysteries. It was the **mystic Tau** of the Chaldeans and Egyptians --- the true original form of **the letter T**, the initial of the name of **Tammuz**, which, in Hebrew, radically the same as ancient Chaldee, as found on coins. **Tau** was marked in baptism on the <u>foreheads</u> of those initiated in the Mysteries and was used in every variety of ways as a most sacred symbol. The mystic **Tau**, as the symbol of the great divinity, was called "the sign of life." The letter T is formed by touching the chest areas at three ends of the T letter (of which an imaginary line could be drawn from the three points). The sign was used as an amulet (charm) over the heart; it was marked on the official garment of the priest; the vestal virgins of pagan Rome wore it suspended from their necklaces, as the nuns do now. The Egyptians did the same.

➤ **<u>Bright light in cults and the occult:</u>**

"Doves of light" were seen flying above the virgin's head. Archaeological discoveries of images of Astart, Cybele, and Isis have the identical dove on their head. This phenomenon is based on the Babylonian trinity (Father, Son, and Mother), in which the female replaces the Holy Ghost (the dove). See *Babylon Mystery Religion,* Ralph Woodrow, p. 25 and *The Two Babylons*, A. Hislop, p. 263.

"Light" or hallucinations of light is commonly reported in occult initiation.

- ✓ "I saw a light" in Zeitoun, Egypt.
- ✓ "A bright light" in Knock, Ireland.
- ✓ "Radiated a brilliant light" in Fatima, Portugal.
- ✓ "Came upon a brilliant light" in La Salette.
- ✓ "Saw a white light about the size of a human" in Banneus, Belgium.
- ✓ "Bright light" in Hercegovinak Yugoslavia.
- ✓ "Saw a brilliant light" in Guadalupe, Mexico.

➤ **<u>Vestal virgin</u>**

Vestal virgin is a virgin consecrated to Vesta, the goddess of fire, and to the service of watching the sacred fire, which was to be perpetually kept burning upon her altar. The Vestals were six in number, and they made a vow of perpetual virginity.

> ## **Hollywood cesspool's favorite religion:**

Has the reader ever noticed how religion is portrayed in Hollywood movies? Anytime a Hollywood movie portrays what they perceive as a "good" religion or a "genuine" preacher, you will be sure to see the "sign of the cross." Conversely, their "bad" religion is always portrayed as a Bible-thumping fundamentalist in the color of fallen preachers or some heretic. Hollywood designed the movie Elmer Gantry to promote this idea in the minds of the populace but are very careful not to expose beer-guzzling drunken sodomite clergymen. Would the reader really expect otherwise from Helly-wood? Any observer with common sense does not have to be a deep thinker to guess what religion the worldly producers and directors favor. Actually, this writer would be shocked if it were any other way! If the reader does not comprehend where the writer is coming from, he is either biased, uninformed, or very naïve.

It appears that television's boob-tube is having an equal influence upon the masses of people even as the Hollywood theaters. Many Christians even name their babies after soap opera stars (the writer has always admired black Americans for naming their children after Bible characters). Usually, soap operas feature ugly souls with attractive bodies. The script is nearly always dirty with a cheating spouse or immoral single. The worldly dress styles and perverted actions of the so-called successful entertainers are emulated by Christians and "professing" Christians.

> ## ➢ **<u>Politically Correct TV reporters are not good spiritual guides:</u>**

The writer was somewhat startled to hear ABC TV's star, Diane Sawyer, exhibit surprising shock because a missionary stated that people of non-Christian faiths (Buddhists, Hindu, Islam, etc.) do not go to Heaven. Diane appeared greatly disturbed that the missionary that she was interviewing (**Jim Bowers**) believed that salvation is only in the **person** of Jesus Christ – (*Prime Time*, ABC Television, May 24, 2001). The writer concedes that Diane was sincere even if sincerely wrong. However, the writer does not reserve the same sentiment for apostate religious leaders who espouse the same false philosophy as Diane's.

(**NOTE:** the writer believes that most false religionists are sincere to some degree to their beliefs. This is clearly demonstrated by the zeal of the Moonies, Muslims, Mormons, Jehovah Witnesses, and Catholics – [Catholics are great humanitarians]. However, sincerity in a false way to Heaven offers no spiritual security. **Jesus Christ** (plus nothing) **is the only way – John 14:6**. Many Baptists, Methodist, Presbyterians, Pentecostals, Charismatics [as well as false religionists] that are trusting in their church affiliation, good works, baptism, communion, gifts of the Spirit, etc., will be greatly shocked at a future time when they are consigned to everlasting fire.)

> ***Matthew 7:21-23:*** *Not everyone that saith unto me, Lord, Lord, shall enter into the kingdom of heaven; but <u>he that doeth the will of my Father</u> which is in heaven. Many will say to me in that day, Lord, Lord, have we not prophesied in thy name? and in thy name have cast out devils? And in thy name done many wonderful works? And then will I profess unto them, I never knew you; depart from me, ye that work iniquity.*

What is the will of the Father?

> ***John 6:40:*** *And this is **the will of him that sent me**, that every one which seeth **the Son**, and believeth on him, may have everlasting life; and I will raise him up at the last day.*

See Ephesians 2:8-9; Galatians 2:16; Romans 3:20, 28; 4:4-6; 10:9-10, 13, 17.

> **The peace symbol**

(The peace symbol is an inverted cross with broken arms encased within a circle)

Militant peace-mongers have sought to have peace even if they had to ruin the other person's peace to get it. The peace symbol used is an ancient symbol used by Satanists, anti-God rebels, communists, and the Roman forces under General Titus Vespasian (later, Emperor Titus).

◆ <u>This peace symbol has been displayed by:</u>

    -Marxist revolutionaries

    -Communist Black Panthers

    -Catholic priests

    -Red-blooded Americans

◆ <u>The peace symbol has been called by many names:</u>

    -The Nero Cross

    -The Sign of the Broken Jew

    -Symbol of the Anti-Christ

    -The Crow's Foot

    -The Witch's foot

    -An Insignia of Satan

Lenin's definition of the term "peace" was, *As an ultimate objective 'peace' simply means Communist world control.* Several major false religions also have the same goal, "world domination." The communists will not reach their goal (Ezekiel 38, 39) but the king of fierce countenance (antichrist beast) will briefly rule the world during the Great Tribulation period using **peace** to destroy many.

> ***Revelation 6:2:*** *And I saw, and behold a white horse: and he that sat on him had **a bow**; and a crown was given unto him: and he went forth conquering and to conquer.*

> ## ➢ A Bow

A bow without an arrow is considered a sham of peace.

> ***Daniel 8:25:*** *And through his policy also he shall cause craft to prosper in his hand; and he shall magnify himself in his heart, and **by peace shall destroy many**: he shall also stand up against the Prince of princes; but he shall be broken without hand.*

◆ The Peace symbol's origin may be traced to 67 AD when **Nero** designed and constructed an upside down broken cross on which he crucified and burned the Apostle Peter.

◆ The peace symbol was adopted in the dark ages by the **Satanists** in an attempt to make mockery of the teachings of Christ.

◆ Today, the peace symbol is used by the **Communists.** What antichrist forces will adopt this symbol next? Antichrist himself?

(copied from *the booklet "PEACE"* by Raymond Blanton of *Highways & Hedges Tracts,* Easley, S.C.)

Again, the Communists will never reach their goal of world conquest but they will reach their end when they go after Israel's mineral wealth (**Ezekiel 38, 39**).

Some think that the peace symbol will be the mark of the beast during The Tribulation Period:

> ***Revelation 13:16-17:*** *And he causeth all, both small and great, rich and poor, free and bond, to receive **a mark** in their right hand, or in their foreheads: And that no man might buy or sell, save he that had **the mark**, or the name of the beast, or the number of his name.*

In the 16th Century, **John Knox** called the peace symbol the mark of the beast.

> ***Isaiah 48:22:*** *There is **no peace**, saith the Lord, unto the wicked.*

Genuine peace is only obtainable in Jesus Christ.

> ***Romans 5:1:*** *Therefore being justified by faith we have **peace** with God through our Lord Jesus Christ.*

> ***Isaiah 9:6:*** *"...His name shall be called Wonderful, Counsellor, The mighty God, The everlasting Father, The **Prince of peace**."*

Today, the peace symbol has become very fashionable. Even Christians no longer speak out against its evil symbolism as they once did. The writer does not believe that God looks upon it favorably when His people adorn themselves with jewelry that sports the peace symbol. Of course, some still do not know its significance. The writer has noticed that when some (even professing Christians) are shown the peace symbol's meaning, they show little or no concern. Surely we are in the Laodicean church age.

Identifying icons of false religions:

There are numerous practices of false religions that identify them as a false way – **Psalms** 119:104; **Proverbs** 14:12; 16:25.

Many people bow down before **images, statues, or icons** which is expressly forbidden by Scriptures.

> ***Exodus 20:4-5:*** *"Thou shalt not make unto thee **any graven image**, or **any likeness of any thing** that is in heaven above, or that is in the earth beneath, or that is in the water under the earth. **Thou shalt not bow down thyself to them**…"*

Also see **Lev.** 26:1; **Deut.** 4:23, 24.

> ***Deuteronomy 4:12, 15, 16:*** *And the LORD spake unto you out of the midst of the fire: ye heard the voice of the words, but saw **no similitude**: only ye heard a voice. Take ye therefore good heed unto yourselves; for ye saw **no manner of similitude** on the day that the LORD spake unto you in Horeb out of the midst of the fire: Lest ye corrupt yourselves, and make you a **graven image**, the similitude of any figure, the likeness of male or female.*

- **Idolaters** shall not inherit the kingdom of God – I Corinthians 6:9.

- **Idolaters** shall have their part in the lake which burneth with fire and brimstone – **Revelation 21:8.**

- **Idolaters** are classed with dogs, sorcerers, murderers, liars and whoremongers – **Revelation 22:15.**

➤ <u>What is an idolater?</u>

Answer: *Websters New World College Dictionary*, Fourth Edition says, a person who worships an idol or idols; a devotee admirer; adorer; showing excessive admiration or devotion; worship idols.

The writer adds that bowing before objects, statues, icons, and images is analogous to using a "go-between" or contact point to God (or a god). Why would bowing before an image or statue of Mary merit favor before God? Why would kissing the toe of Peter's statue merit favor before God? Why would kissing the pope's toe merit favor before God? This is no more than "object lesson" idolatry as demonstrated when the children of Israel did burn incense to the brazen serpent (2 Kings 18:4). The brasen serpent was a symbol of sin judged and life given, not an image representative of the true and living God. Of course, the Israelites sinned in the matter of the idolatrous molten calf (Exodus 32:4, 8, 23). God does not expect us to worship Him through icons, objects, images, and statues.

➢ **The great vanity of Israel was in the pride of idols:**

> *Jeremiah 18:15: Because my people hath forgotten me, they have burned incense to vanity (idols) and they have cause them to stumble in their ways from the ancient paths, to walk in paths, in a way not cast up.*

The "ancient paths" were appointed by Divine Law:

> *Exodus 20:4-5: thou shalt not make unto thee **any graven image**, or **any likeness of any thing** that is in heaven above, or that is in the earth beneath, or that is in the water under the earth: **Thou shalt not bow down thyself to them**, nor serve them: for I the LORD thy God am a jealous God, visiting the iniquity of the fathers upon the children unto the third and fourth generation of them that hate me.*

➢ **What is the proper way to worship God?**

> *John 4:24: God is a Spirit: and they that worship him must worship him in spirit and in truth.*

Images and figures were forbidden to the Jews many times in the Old Testament. Idolatry (images, icons, etc.) is the highest form of insult to Deity.

Refer to **Acts** 7:39-42; **Acts** 17:16, 29; **Romans** 1:23; **I Corinthians** 10:7, 14; **I**

Corinthians 12:2; **I Peter** 4:3; **Revelation** 2:14; **Revelation** 9:20

➢ Babylonian idolatry of icons, images, and relics abounds in our modern era of advanced technology

<u>EXAMPLES</u>:
- The Shroud of Turin
- Veneration of the dead
- Bowing down before images
- Bleeding statues
- Statues of Mary and "so-called" saints
- Weeping pictures or statues
- Apparitions of Mary
- Wood from the cross of Christ
- Peter's bones
- Certain hallowed locations (as hallowed fields and sanctuaries "so-called")

➢ Shroud of Turin:

A French magazine says it has carried out experiments that prove the Shroud of Turin is a fake. The Shroud is claimed by defenders to be the cloth in which the body of Jesus Christ was wrapped after His crucifixion. It bears the faint image of a blood-covered man with holes in his hands and wounds in his body and head, the apparent result of being crucified, stabbed by a Roman spear and forced to wear a crown of thorns.

In 1988, scientists carried out Carbon-14 dating of the cloth and concluded that the material was made sometimes between 1260 and 1390. This prompted the then archbishop of Turin, where the Shroud is stored, to admit that the garment was a hoax - *The Sword of the Lord*, 10-07-05.

There are other scientific documentations exposing the phony Shroud.

NOTE: In March 2008, the writer happened across a Christian TV program (Channel 16 of Greenville, S. C.) in which a gentleman gave a long presentation in favor of the authenticity of The Shroud of Turin. I do not question this man's salvation nor the genuineness of his sincerity, but I certainly do not agree with his view of the shroud. I do not judge a man's Christian character if he chooses to believe in some relic but I reserve the right to disagree. Come to think of it, could a shroud be indelibly marked for nearly two-thousand years after only three days lying loosely upon a body that was already prepared, cleansed, and wound in linen (John 19:40)? There is no mention of a shroud in the sepulcher, but there was a napkin that was about his head, not lying with the linen clothes but wrapped together in a place by itself (John 20:7). The Word of God is all the proof we need!

➢ <u>Buddha's tooth</u>

Even Buddha's tooth is considered sacred. There are many religious relics and practices. (Refer to **Exodus** 20:4, 5; **Leviticus** 26:1; **Deuteronomy** 4:12-19, 23-24).

CHAPTER 6

NUMBERS, NUMBERS, AND MORE NUMBERS

In today's consumer market, most of our purchased goods have bar codes representing their cost in dollars and cents of amounts (numbers).

- Our **telephone** numbers have an area code number.
- Our **residence** has a zip code number.
- Our **employee earnings** are assigned a social security number.
- The same **social security number** is now given to us at birth whereas it was formerly given us at employment age.
- **Military men** now use their social security number instead of an assigned military number.
- Our **bills** and invoices all have numbers.
- Even **prison inmates** have long been given a number equated to a name.

- All banking cards and credit cards have private assigned numbers.

Numbers and marks are associated with about everything (serial numbers; tag numbers; ID numbers; model numbers; etc.). Of course, this is all leading to the time of the Tribulation Period when all people will be compelled to receive a mark, name of the beast, or the number of the beast **in** (not, "on") their right hand or **in** their forehead in order to buy or sell. If any refuse to worship the beast, they will be killed (**Revelation 13:15**). Probably most who refuse the mark of the beast will be slain by the sword or guillotine - (**Revelation 20:4**). Those who receive the mark of the beast will damn their own souls, completely alienating themselves from the mercy of God (**Revelation 14:9--11**).

There have been numerous candidates for the person alleged to fit the role of Antichrist. There are too many candidates based upon **gematria** (numerical value of name equivalent to 666) to have any real meaning.

(**gematria** = numerical values of alphabet letters added together and corresponding to a certain total value. Greek alphabet "alpha" = 1; "beta" = 2; etc.)

(**NOTE:** Some think that the mark of the beast of **Revelation 13** represents 18 digits or that the number 6 multiplied by the number of times of occurrence is equivalent to 666 (or, 3 X 6 = 18). They translate this to mean everyone will be assigned an 18-digit world number in an implanted microchip (by a hypodermic needle). In this way, everyone can be identified and located by satellite **GPS** [Global Positioning System]. <u>Example</u>: World National number, as 0008; Zip Code number, as 29000; Social Security Number, as 250-00-0000. These arbitrary digits add up to 18.)

The Mark of the Beast: Revelation 13

The writer does not believe that the doom of those who receive the mark of the beast (in order to do business during the Tribulation Period) is attributable to simply receiving a mark or number to conduct business. Receiving this mark has a much deeper religious or spiritual meaning. The writer believes that the true meaning of the reception of the beast-mark or number is an acknowledgement of a false messiah, the man of sin, as Messiah (**John 5:43; 2 Thessalonians 2:10-12**). The reception of the mark appears to be a philosophical and spiritual acceptance of the antichrist that is a form of blasphemy paralleled in the Gospels. For example, the unbelieving Jews attributed the "wonderful works" of the Spirit of God to demonic power (**Matthew 12:28-32**). This was considered blasphemy against the Holy Spirit and was never to be forgiven. In a dissimilar way the "wicked workings" of Satan and the demonic forces during the Tribulation Period are attributed to Messiah by those that accept the mark of the beast. The acceptance of the mark of the beast preserves the physical life of the deluded souls a little longer but seals their eternal damnation **(Revelation 14:9-11)**.

➤ Bar Codes

When bar codes first began to be used in grocery stores, many people began associating it to the mark of the beast of Revelation chapter 13. Presently, the use of bar codes is so common in stores that one barely notices them any more. One writer says that there are three different types of bar codes for use in different types of industries. Another writer says that three of the vertical bars are equivalent to the numerical value of 666 (three 6's = 666). No wonder there was concern for some!

Our government does not please to educate us on bar codes so it is up to us to inform ourselves since some of us do not prefer to buy products from China.

The following table lists codes numbers identifying the country where the product is manufactured (first digits):

00-09 - USA & CANADA

30-37 - FRANCE

40-44 - GERMANY

49 – JAPAN

50 – UK

471 - TAIWAN

690-692 – CHINA (first three digits of the bar code)

Although the bar codes are not the mark of the beast of Revelation 13, they sure do remind us of the technology that is already in place to enable the fulfillment of Revelation 13. An implanted microchip in a person's forehead or right hand can easily accomplish the soul-damning, "…mark, or the name of the beast, or the number of his name" (Revelation 13:17).

Of course, there is always a good humanitarian reason for implanting the microchips. "All of Satan's apples have worms," as someone has stated.

-Police can track and locate stolen cars.

-Pets and animals can be found.

-Alzheimer patients can be quickly located.

-Personal health data can be stored within the chip (diabetic; allergies; blood type).

-Abducted children can be rescued...

And the list of good things generated by implanted microchips goes on and on.

Imitation By Satan

In imitation of the Holy Trinity or "Tri-Unity" of God (Father, Son, and Holy Ghost), Satan emulates God in an "unholy trinity" (dragon or devil, beast, and false prophet – **Revelation** 16:13; 19:20; 20:10). Satan attempts to damn souls of men by cleverly imitating true religion by *a way that seemeth right unto a man"* (**Proverbs** 14:12; 16:25), but it is a false way (**John** 14:6). Jesus alone is the true way and Satan tries to supplant God's truth with a lie (a false way). This is particularly true in religion. In **Revelation 17**, we see the religious whore (Babylon) riding upon the back of the One-World Political System. There has **only been one** phony *religion* that has controlled world governments for centuries and has slain millions of Christians under the color of law and under the guise (or, "cover") of religion. True martyrs for Jesus were falsely branded as heretics by the phony state religion. GUESS WHO!

Perhaps the reader should read Foxes Book of Martyrs, Trail of the Blood, and Baptist History.

➤ <u>The Holy Spirit</u>

The spiritual and invisible **seal** of the safety of a saved person's soul is illustrated by the **seal** of the Holy Spirit. He is the believer's security:

> ***Ephesians 1:13:*** *In whom ye also trusted, after that ye heard the word of truth, the gospel of your salvation: in whom also after that ye believed, ye were **sealed** with that holy **Spirit** of promise*

> ***Ephesians 4:30:*** *And grieve not the holy **Spirit** of God, whereby ye are **sealed** unto the day of redemption.*

> ***2 Corinthians 1:22:*** *Who hath **sealed** us, and given the earnest of the **Spirit** in our hearts.*

> ***Hebrews 13:5:*** *Let your conversation be with out covetousness; and be content with such things as ye have: for he hath said, I will <u>never leave thee, nor forsake thee</u>.*

> ***John 6:37:*** *All that the Father giveth me shall come to me; and him that cometh to me I will <u>in no wise cast out</u>.*

> ***John 10:27-29:*** *My sheep hear my voice, and I know them, and they follow me: And I give unto them eternal life; and they shall <u>never perish</u>, neither shall any man pluck them out of my hand. My Father, which gave them me, is greater than all; and no man is able to pluck them out of my Father's hand.*

> ***Romans 8:37-39:*** *For I am persuaded, that neither death, nor life, nor angels, nor; principalities, nor powers, nor things present, nor things to come, Nor height, nor*

depth, nor any other creature, shall be able to separate us form the love of God, which is in Christ Jesus our Lord.

Conclusion

Many events in the end-time may be of a supernatural nature of demonic deception. The masses of people (even in Christendom) are very subject to impressions of the supernatural element. People want to "see" something! Many will travel miles to see an alleged healing or miracle (as a wart removed). The Word of God does not satisfy them. Again, they want to see and "feel" something! During The Tribulation Period, the beast out of the earth will do great wonders and make fire come down from heaven on the earth in the sight of men, and deceive them that dwell on the earth by the means of those miracles which he had power to do in the sight of the beast...**(Revelation 13:13-14)**.

Elements of the satanic world do an excellent job in keeping their secrets hidden by using codes, signs, symbols, marks, icons, etc. Most of these symbols are constantly before us in plain sight daily. Awake out of thy sleep, Christian!

*Matthew 7:22-23: Many will say to me in that day, Lord, Lord, have we not prophesied in thy name? and in thy name have **cast out devils**? And in thy name **done many wonderful works?** And them* *will I profess unto them, I never knew you; depart from me, ye that work iniquity.*

Look around and see who these people are that are seeking signs and claiming miracles!

Matthew 12:39: *But He answered and said unto them,* **An evil and adulterous generation seeketh after a sign**; *and there shall no sign be given to it, but the sign of the prophet Jonas –*

Romans 13:12: The night is far spent and the day is at hand: let us therefore cast off the works of darkness, and let us put on the armour of light.

ABOUT THE AUTHOR

 The writer was born in Greenville, SC in 1934 and was a lifetime resident except for two years in the US Army (Fort Jackson, S.C. and Fort Carson, Colorado) and two years residence in Florida.

After separation (honorably) from the US Army, the writer returned to Greenville, SC and married at age 27 to Christine Moore, an old acquaintance from an adjacent neighborhood. The Lord blessed us with six daughters, Debbie, Donna, Dale, Denise, Deree, and Dena.

A short time after marriage, the writer was convicted of his lost condition as a sinner and after a miserable time under conviction the writer confessed his sin and lost condition to God and was saved.

The writer was 40 years of age when he began attending college (3 years, no diploma).

The writer retired as a chemical technologist from Morton International Chemical Company in 1996. Before retirement, the writer had the urge to write on Bible subjects and wished that he had more time to study. Upon retirement, the writer bought a computer and became a novice writer.

The writer now resides in Easley, S.C.

D. Helton has written several documents and books, as well as the books or booklets: "Jesus is God," "Evolution, Another False Religion of Humanism," "Cremation: Christian or Pagan," "Is The Gap Theory Credible?" "Does Water Baptism Save," "Can a Saved Person Become Unsaved," and several others, available here:

http://www.theoldpathspublications.com/Pages/Authors/Helton.htm#God

Dennis Helton
200 Home Place Drive
Easley, SC 29640